the Happy
CAMPER
· COOKBOOK ·

ISBN-13: 978-1-56383-576-6
Item #2920

Printed in the USA
Distributed By:

507 Industrial Street
Waverly, IA 50677

www.cqbookstore.com

gifts@cqbookstore.com

 CQ Products

 CQ Products

 @cqproducts

 @cqproducts

Happy Camper Hacks

1. At home, cook and shred a bunch of meat. Take along for sandwiches, tacos, soups, and anything else your campers like.

2. Before you leave, whisk some eggs and transfer them to a water bottle for no-break transport and easy usage once you arrive.

3. Heat one end of plastic straws to seal. Pour in small amounts of seasonings and seal the other end. Use a marker to label.

4. Cut up fresh veggies – they're great as a quick side dish or simply for snacking.

5. Consider fruits that travel well *(apples, oranges, whole melons)*. Canned fruit is easy to pack and you won't crush the contents *(don't forget the can opener)*.

6. Use frozen gallon jugs of water in your cooler instead of ice to keep things cold longer.

7. Take along plenty of foil; use it for cooking, lining grill grates, and even scraping dirty pans *(scrunch the foil into a ball first)*.

8. Burn bundles of fresh sage at the edge of your campfire to help repel mosquitoes.

9. Sprinkle sprigs of fresh herbs over hot coals, adding herb-infused smoke to your grilled food.

Breakfast burritos are a camping staple – or they should be. Easily tote-able, they make the perfect take-along. Make up a bunch and stash them in your freezer until needed.

Tot-a-licious Breakfast Burritos

2 C. frozen mini tater tots

8 breakfast sausage patties

2 T. olive oil

8 eggs, beaten

⅓ C. half & half

Salt and black pepper to taste

1 (16 oz.) can refried beans *(or use black beans, drained & rinsed)*

8 (8") flour tortillas, heated as directed on pkg.

2 C. shredded Mexican cheese blend

2 Roma tomatoes, chopped

¼ C. chopped fresh cilantro

NEEDED AT CAMP

Toppings: sour cream, diced tomatoes, cilantro

Before you Go

Bake tater tots according to package directions. Don't turn off the oven when they're done, but make sure to reset it if needed to 400°.

Meanwhile, in a big skillet over medium-high heat, cook the sausage patties in hot oil, chopping them while they cook; remove the sausage and drain all but about 1 tablespoon of the grease from the skillet. Add the eggs and cook until just barely beginning to set, whisking often. Slowly whisk in the half & half and season with salt and pepper. Continue cooking until eggs are completely set.

Spread the refried beans evenly down the middle of the tortillas and top with tater tots, sausage, eggs, cheese, tomatoes, and cilantro. Roll up burrito-style and place seam side down on a lightly greased baking sheet; cover with foil and bake 12 to 15 minutes, until heated through and the tortillas are a little crisp and lightly browned. Let cool.

Wrap each cooled burrito in heavy-duty foil, tuck them into a big zippered plastic bag, and keep 'em chilled *(or freeze them first)*.

At Camp

Reheat individual burritos in foil in the hot coals or on the grill. Toss on any toppings you'd like.

Got mac & cheese lovers? Add this to your camping food rotation and you'll be the coolest cook in the campground.

Alfredo Mac & Cheese

1½ C. uncooked elbow macaroni

1 C. prepared Alfredo sauce

½ C. shredded sharp cheddar cheese

½ C. grated Parmesan cheese

¼ C. shredded mozzarella cheese

Salt and black pepper to taste

¼ to ½ C. half & half

Crumbled bacon

NEEDED AT CAMP

Half & half or milk

Before you Go

Spritz an 8" foil pie pan with cooking spray and set aside.

Cook macaroni according to package directions; drain and rinse. Stir in the Alfredo sauce, cheddar, Parmesan, mozzarella, salt, and pepper. Stir in enough half & half to make things nice and saucy. Transfer the mixture to the prepped pan, toss on the bacon, and cover tightly with foil that has also been spritzed with cooking spray; keep cool.

At Camp

Reheat covered mac & cheese on a rack over hot coals or on a grill until heated through, adding a little half & half or milk if needed to increase moisture. Serve immediately.

Serves 4-6

Make part of this beast at home — it will keep well for several days.
Add more yummy toppings at your destination and dive in.

Slice-and-Share Hoagie

- 1 garlic clove
- 6 pickled cherry peppers
- 2 T. chopped pepperoncini peppers
- 1 T. white wine vinegar
- 1 tsp. sugar
- 12" to 16" hoagie roll or unsliced Italian bread loaf
- 12 to 15 slices of your favorite lunch meats *(we used a combo of salami, pickle & pimento loaf, and Canadian Bacon)*
- 4 to 5 slices provolone cheese
- 2 T. mayo

NEEDED AT CAMP

Toppings: tomato slices, shredded lettuce, Italian seasoning, red wine vinegar, olive oil

Before you Go

Finely chop the garlic and all the peppers and mix with the vinegar and sugar; cover and chill until needed.

Split the hoagie roll horizontally without cutting all the way through; spread on the mayo and layer on the lunch meat and cheese. Set the top half of the bun in place and wrap the whole thing tightly in plastic wrap; chill.

At Camp

When you're ready to eat, spread the chilled pepper mixture on the sandwich. Add tomato and lettuce. Sprinkle with Italian seasoning and drizzle with a little vinegar and oil if you'd like. Slice and eat promptly.

Mocha Dust Nuts

Microwave 1 C. dark chocolate chips until melted. Stir in 2 C. toasted whole almonds until coated. In a big bowl, combine ¾ C. powdered sugar, 3 T. unsweetened cocoa powder, and 1½ T. instant coffee granules. Add the chocolate-coated almonds and toss to coat. Spread in a single layer on a waxed paper-lined baking sheet and chill until set. Transfer to an airtight container and keep cool.

9

Why are these called Happy Camper Parfaits? Customization, folks. Everybody gets what they like, but there's no extra work involved. Simple and yummy.

Happy Camper Fruit Parfaits

At Camp: For each parfait, stir together a 6 oz. container yogurt *(any flavor)* and ¼ C. quick-cooking oats. Layer yogurt mixture in a wide-mouth half-pint or 1-pint mason jar along with ¼ to 1 C. add-ins* *(depending on the size of jar)* to correspond with the flavor of yogurt being used. There's no wrong combination. Enjoy immediately or cover and chill up to 5 days.

* *Add-in inspiration: raspberry yogurt, fresh raspberries, raspberry jam; pineapple-coconut yogurt, canned pineapple chunks (drained), sliced almonds, toasted coconut; lemon yogurt, fresh blackberries, crushed graham crackers; apple-cinnamon yogurt, chopped pecans, chunky applesauce; vanilla yogurt, frozen cherries, dark chocolate chunks*

Serves 4

Shrimp feels like a special treat when you're camping. Don't ruin the mood by burning yourself with steam when you open the foil packs. Mind your fingers!

Shrimp Foil Packs

Before you Go: In a glass bowl, microwave 1 lb. halved small red potatoes and 4 frozen mini chunks sweet corn for 8 to 10 minutes, until just tender. When cool, stir in 2 tsp. canola oil and 1 tsp. Old Bay seasoning and transfer to a covered container. Slice 13 oz. andouille sausage into a separate container; in a third container, combine 12 oz. raw shrimp *(peeled & deveined)* and 1 tsp. Old Bay seasoning. Cover containers and keep chilled.

At Camp: Spritz four big sheets of heavy-duty foil with cooking spray and divide the sausage, corn, potatoes, and shrimp evenly among them. Put lemon wedges on top. Fold the foil around the food, creating sealed packs; cook over medium heat on a grill or on a rack above hot coals until shrimp are pink. Squeeze lemons over the food.

Fried rice in the morning? Absolutely! It has all the elements of an absolutely delicious day-starter.

Fried Rice for Breakfast

2 C. white and/or brown rice

6 breakfast sausage links

4 green onions, sliced

3 T. sesame oil

Soy sauce to taste

NEEDED AT CAMP

4 eggs

Salt and black pepper

Before you Go

Cook rice in boiling water according to package directions until tender and the water is absorbed. In the meantime, cook the sausages until done, chopping them while they cook; drain the grease. Set both aside to cool.

Stir the rice, sausage, and green onions together and transfer to a covered container. Combine the oil and soy sauce in a separate container; cover and keep cool.

At Camp

Whisk the eggs and pour into a big greased skillet over the fire or on a grill, breaking them apart while they cook. Stir in the chilled rice and oil mixtures. Heat until browned and crusty on the bottom; scrape up the browned bits, stir and heat until everything is nice and hot. Season with salt and pepper.

Funky S'mores

Lemon-Lemon

lemon curd, cookies & cream candy bar, and toasted marshmallows between two lemon cookies

Party Pastry

milk chocolate candy bar, toasted pink marshmallows, and rainbow sprinkles between a split toaster pastry *(ours was chocolate sundae-flavored)*

Cinnamon Sensation

dark chocolate candy bar, a sprinkle of cayenne pepper, and toasted marshmallows between a split cinnamon-sugar cake donut

Minty Mix

mint chocolate candy, toasted marshmallows, and crushed peppermints between a pair of graham crackers

No frying necessary. Just get out the pie irons and in a few minutes, you'll have corn dogs that'll make your gang howl.

Quick Corn Dogs

At Camp: Cook 4 hot dogs or small brats *(plain or cheese-filled)* over the fire or on the grill, then thinly slice them; set aside. Spray pie irons heavily with cooking spray. Stir together 1 (8.5 oz.) pkg. corn muffin mix, 1 egg, and ⅓ C. milk. For each corn dog, scoop enough batter into one side of a pie iron to just cover the bottom. Arrange some of the sliced hot dogs or brats over the top and drizzle with BBQ sauce and/or yellow mustard; cover with batter. Close the iron and cook slowly over hot coals until batter is cooked, turning occasionally until toasty brown on both sides.

This is about the most convenient light meal imaginable for a camping trip. Try the ideas here or come up with your own twists – the options are nearly endless.

Instant Noodle Jar Soup

Flavor base *(such as soup stock paste, tahini, or curry paste)*

Extra flavorings *(such as chili sauce, soy sauce, Worcestershire sauce, or coconut milk)*

Fillers *(such as frozen veggies, diced tofu, leftover cooked meat, thinly sliced mushrooms, or hard-cooked eggs)*

Cooked noodles *(such as ramen, spaghetti, or rice noodles)*

Fresh ingredients *(such as herbs, sliced green onions, diced peppers, bean sprouts, lime slices)*

Seasonings *(such as salt, black pepper, garlic powder, seasoned salt, lemon pepper)*

Before you Go

For each serving, spread up to 1 tablespoon flavor base in the bottom of a single serving container with a lid *(a wide-mouth 1-pint mason jar works really well for this – the screw-on lid keeps everything inside, plus you can clearly see the ingredients).*

Next add up to 1 tablespoon of extra flavorings. Use whatever sounds good to you.

Scatter up to ½ cup of fillers over the top – have fun with variety here.

Now add ¾ to 1 cup cooked noodles, packing down relatively tightly *(don't worry if they stick together).*

Top it off with up to ½ cup of your favorite fresh ingredients.

Season to taste, seal the jar, and refrigerate up to 1 week.

At Camp

When you're ready to eat, pour enough boiling water into the jar to just cover the ingredients; seal the jar and set aside about 5 minutes, then stir thoroughly.

Munch Munch

Before you go, mix equal amounts of the following ingredients in a zippered plastic bag or airtight container: salted pepitas, sunflower kernels, yogurt- or chocolate-covered raisins, dried fruit, and unsweetened coconut chips (toasted if desired). Mix it up, take it along, and enjoy.

A ton of sweet deliciousness crammed into each pack. Dinner never tasted so good.

Honeyed Pork & Veggie Packs

¼ C. brown sugar

½ C. honey

4 boneless pork chops

Salt and black pepper to taste

2 (16 oz.) pkgs. frozen stir-fry vegetables, thawed

At Camp

Spritz four big sheets of heavy-duty foil with cooking spray. In a bowl, stir together the brown sugar and honey.

Sprinkle both sides of the pork chops with salt and pepper and set each one on a sheet of the foil. Divide the honey mixture evenly among the chops. Arrange the vegetables over and around each chop and sprinkle with more salt and pepper.

Wrap the foil around the food, sealing everything inside and cook over medium heat on a covered grill or over coals until the meat is done and the vegetables are tender. Open the packs carefully.

Puff pastry turns magical when it's baked, becoming crispy on the outside, cloud-like in the middle, and buttery throughout. Add pie filling for a combination that's out of this world.

Fruit Puffs

At Camp: Spritz pie irons with cooking spray. Press or roll 2 thawed puff pastry sheets until thin; cut to fit the pie irons *(you should be able to cut four to six squares from each sheet)*. Position one square inside an iron. Put a big scoop of your favorite pie filling on the pastry, spreading out close to the edges. Add in a spoonful of extras if you'd like *(try raisins with apple filling, blueberries with lemon, white chocolate baking chips with cherry)*. Cover with another puff pastry square. Close the pie iron and cook over warm coals until the pastry is golden brown on both sides, turning occasionally. *(Note: puff pastry expands as it cooks, so open carefully when checking for doneness.)*

Makes about 1½ cups

This protein-packed dip is a surefire way to make sure everyone's eating their fruit. Bonus: this ultra-decadent dip is actually HEALTHY and a no-guilt way to get your chocolate fix!

Chocolate-Peanut Butter Hummus

Before you Go: In a food processor, combine 1 (16 oz.) can chickpeas *(drained & rinsed)*, ¼ C. peanut butter, ¼ C. plus 1 T. pure maple syrup, ½ C. unsweetened cocoa powder, 1 tsp. vanilla, and ¼ tsp. salt. Process for 30 seconds, then scrape down the sides of the bowl. Add 2 to 3 T. water and process again until it becomes nice and creamy; chill.

At Camp: Set the hummus aside for a bit to soften, then stir. Drizzle with maple syrup and top with chopped peanuts. Serve with pretzels and fresh fruit *(we used apples and strawberries)*.

Sometimes nothing tastes better than a bowl of oatmeal. Combine the mixture at home and tote it along; in the morning, it takes only 5 minutes to prepare. Adapt it to suit your taste.

DIY Instant Oatmeal

6 C. old-fashioned oats

2 C. of your favorite dried fruit *(we used a combo of cherries, cranberries, and chopped banana chips)*

½ C. brown sugar

¾ tsp. salt

NEEDED AT CAMP

Milk

Toppings: brown sugar, vanilla yogurt, chocolate chips, coconut, nuts, and/or other favorites

Before you Go

In a big bowl, combine oats, dried fruit, brown sugar, and salt. Mix with your hands until the fruit no longer sticks together. Store in an airtight container until needed. Pack toppings separately.

At Camp

For each serving, put ¾ cup of the oatmeal mixture into a bowl and add ¾ cup boiling water; cover and set aside for 5 minutes until most of the water has been absorbed.

Drizzle in some milk and add toppings of your choice.

Ooey-gooey and absolutely taco-licious, this favorite is brimming with mouth-watering goodness. Pass the napkins.

Chicken Taco Pull-Apart

¾ lb. boneless, skinless chicken thighs

2 (.25 oz.) pkgs. taco seasoning, divided

⅔ C. water

4 bacon strips

1 (4.5 oz.) can diced green chiles

7 T. unsalted butter

NEEDED AT CAMP

1 (½ lb.) unsliced round loaf sourdough or ciabatta bread

3 C. shredded Mexican cheese blend, divided

Sliced jalapeños, optional

24

Before you Go

Cook and shred the chicken and toss into a saucepan with 1 package of the taco seasoning and the water; simmer several minutes, until thickened. Cool, then pack into a lidded container. Cook the bacon until nice and crispy; cool and put into a separate container. In a third small container, combine the chiles, butter, and 1½ teaspoons of the remaining taco seasoning; cover. Cover everything and chill.

At Camp

Melt the chilled butter mixture, stirring to combine. Make criss-cross cuts 1" apart deeply into the top of the bread, without cutting all the way through to the bottom. Set the bread on two big sheets of heavy-duty foil and bring the foil up around the sides of the bread, creating a nest.

Stuff 2 cups of the cheese and all the chicken mixture between the cuts. Slowly drizzle the hot butter mixture over the chicken, coating everything evenly. Scatter the jalapeños, bacon, and the remaining 1 cup cheese over the top.

Spritz another sheet of foil with cooking spray and use it to loosely cover the bread. Set on a rack over warm coals or on a grill over low heat until the chicken is hot, the cheese is melted, and everything is nicely toasted.

Single-Serve Homemade Ice Cream

1 T. sugar
½ C. whipping cream
¼ tsp. vanilla
6 T. rock salt

Crushed ice
Optional toppings
  of your choice

At Camp

In a pint- or quart-size zippered freezer bag, combine the sugar, whipping cream, and vanilla; remove excess air, zip closed, and mix well. Tuck the bag into a second bag; remove air and zip closed.

Fill a gallon-size zippered freezer bag halfway with crushed ice; add the rock salt and shake to distribute the salt evenly throughout the ice.

Bury the small bags inside the gallon bag containing the ice. Remove air and zip closed. Wrap a towel around the bag and shake vigorously for 8 to 10 minutes, squeezing and massaging the bag often, until the ice cream is the consistency of soft-serve.

Carefully remove the small bags from the gallon bag and remove the outer small bag. Eat directly out of the inner bag, adding toppings if you'd like.

Better than a drive-thru any day, these breakfast sandwiches are made in a pie iron and packed with flavor. Experiment with your favorite ingredient combos.

Canadian Breakfast Sandwiches

At Camp: Grease a pie iron. For each sandwich, split an English muffin or large baked biscuit and set half in a pie iron. Whisk a small egg and pour it slowly over your bread choice; sprinkle with salt and black pepper. Lay a few Canadian bacon slices over the egg. To make a savory sandwich, drizzle with just a bit of mustard and/or mayo and top with mild cheddar cheese. For something a little sweeter, smear on some orange marmalade or apricot or peach jelly instead. Top with the other muffin or biscuit half. Close the iron and toast over the fire until the egg is cooked.

You CAN eat healthy while you're camping. And with these make-ahead salads, you don't even have to think about it. Just grab and eat.

Salads to Go

Before you Go: In a big bowl, mix 3 C. chopped fresh kale, 1½ C. packaged broccoli slaw, 1 C. chopped cooked chicken, and ⅓ C. dried cranberries. Pour 1 to 2 T. of your favorite salad dressing into the bottom of four wide-mouth 1-pint mason jars or other lidded containers. Divide the salad mixture among the jars and seal with lids.

At Camp: Give the salads a quick stir and toss 2 to 3 T. sunflower kernels or pepitas on top.

The little charred bits created from the heat add a nice subtle smokiness to this corn. You could just serve corn with butter, but you'd be missing out on all that extra yumminess.

Mexican Sweet Corn

8 ears sweet corn
2 limes, cut into wedges
½ C. mayo
1 C. sour cream
¼ C. chopped cilantro

NEEDED AT CAMP
Parmesan cheese
Chili powder to taste

Before you Go

Husk the corn and toss into a zippered plastic bag with the limes. Combine the mayo, sour cream, and cilantro in a small zippered plastic bag. Seal the bag and tuck it inside the bag with the corn and limes; zip closed. Chill until needed.

At Camp

Grill the corn over the campfire or on a grill, turning frequently until slightly charred all the way around.

Remove the corn from the heat and slather with the mayo mixture *(you can simply snip an end off the bag and drizzle the mixture over the corn if you'd like)*. Cool for a few minutes, and then sprinkle each ear with Parmesan cheese and chili powder. Squeeze the lime wedges over the top.

The flavor of these meatballs is reminiscent of old-fashioned pizza burgers, so you know they're gonna be great! And foil packs? What's not to love?!

Pizza Burger Meatballs

1 lb. ground pork

½ lb. ground Italian sausage

1 C. panko bread crumbs

1 egg

½ C. milk

1½ tsp. salt

¼ tsp. dried parsley

3 T. grated Parmesan cheese

¾ tsp. garlic powder

1 (15 oz.) can spaghetti sauce, divided

NEEDED AT CAMP

Remaining spaghetti sauce from above

Fresh mozzarella cheese

Before you Go

In a bowl, combine ground pork, ground sausage, bread crumbs, egg, milk, salt, parsley, Parmesan, garlic powder, and ½ cup spaghetti sauce. Using your hands, mix until just blended; form into 1½" balls and place in a covered container. Pack the remaining spaghetti sauce separately and keep everything cool.

At Camp

Spritz six double-layer squares of foil with cooking spray and spread 1 tablespoon of the remaining spaghetti sauce in the center of each. Divide the meatballs evenly among the foil squares, and drizzle the remaining sauce evenly over the top. Create a packet by folding the edges of the foil together, sealing the meatballs inside, but leaving some open space around them.

Cook on a rack over hot coals or in a covered grill for 15 to 20 minutes or until cooked through, carefully flipping the packets halfway through cooking time.

Open carefully to prevent a painful steam bath for your skin. Toss in some mozzarella and let it melt.

Rainbow Pinwheels

Before you go, mix ⅔ C. whipped cream cheese with 1 T. dry ranch dressing and spread evenly over one side of 2 (10") spinach-herb wraps. Toss together ¼ C. each finely diced carrot and red and yellow bell pepper, ¼ C. chopped baby spinach, and ¼ C. shredded purple cabbage and distribute evenly among the tortillas, leaving a 1" border. Roll up the tortillas tightly, wrap individually in plastic wrap, and chill. Then just slice and serve.
Serves 4

33

Mixing the tomatoes, corn, and black beans with the onion, garlic, and seasonings before you go gives the flavors a chance to mingle. Toss in the avocados just before serving for a burst of freshness.

Corn & Black Bean Guacamole

Before you Go: In an airtight container, combine 1 Roma tomato *(diced)*, ½ red onion *(diced)*, 2 garlic cloves *(minced)*, 1 C. each canned sweet corn and black beans *(drained & rinsed)*, 2 T. lime juice, ½ tsp. each salt and black pepper, ¼ tsp. cayenne pepper, ½ C. chopped fresh cilantro; cover and chill.

At Camp: Peel, pit and mash 3 avocados to desired texture and stir them into the tomato mixture. Serve with tortilla chips.

These make a perfect side dish to just about anything you're eating. They get toasty in the pie iron, and everybody can individualize their own with their favorite veggies, meat, and cheese.

Pie Iron Ranch Browns

At Camp: Coat your pie iron with plenty of cooking spray and pack in a thick layer of thawed shredded hash browns. Sprinkle with a little dry ranch dressing mix and black pepper. Add some chopped green onions and deli ham or salami and spread on about 2 T. sour cream. Top with your favorite shredded cheese. Add another layer of hash browns and pack everything down tightly.

Close the iron and cook on each side for a few minutes, until hash browns are golden brown. Top with sour cream and chives if you'd like.

This is a classic chili recipe that you make at home, then heat up at camp. It doesn't get any easier – or any better – than this.

Campfire Chili

- 2 lbs. ground beef
- 2 lbs. ground pork
- 1 onion, diced
- 2 bell peppers, diced (any color)
- 2 (16 oz.) cans tomato sauce
- 1 (6 oz.) can tomato paste
- 2 (14.5 oz.) cans diced fire-roasted tomatoes
- 1 (15 oz.) can baked beans with brown sugar
- 1 C. beef broth
- 2 tsp. minced garlic
- 2 to 3 T. chili powder
- Salt, black pepper, and ground cumin to taste

Before you Go

Brown the beef and pork, crumbling it while it cooks; drain and cool completely. Dump the cooled meat into a big lidded container and stir in the onion, bell peppers, tomato sauce, tomato paste, tomatoes, baked beans, broth, garlic, chili powder, salt, pepper, and cumin. Cover and chill.

At Camp

Transfer the chili to a big saucepan or Dutch oven. Cover and heat on a grate over the fire or on a grill until bubbly.

Leftover Inspiration

Make chili dogs, ladle over baked potatoes, or add to individual bags of corn chips and top with shredded cheese and lettuce to eat like walking tacos.

Serves 5

A nice appetizer to share while your meal is cooking. It goes together quickly and tastes great.

Simple Cilantro Bruschetta

At Camp: Chop 2 or 3 tomatoes and put them into a bowl with 2 finely chopped garlic cloves, 2 T. chopped cilantro, and salt and black pepper to taste. Drizzle in a little olive oil and stir it all together. Taste and adjust seasonings.

Drizzle both sides of 10 French bread slices with olive oil and set on a grate over a fire or on a hot grill, turning to toast both sides. Remove the bread from the heat and sprinkle with garlic powder. Top with a generous scoop of the tomato mixture.

38

A delicious way to start your day. These individual servings of French toast are made in foil packs, and that means no dirty dishes! Just one more thing to be happy about today.

Berry-Peach French Toast

At Camp: For each serving, tear 2 bread slices into cubes and dump onto a big piece of foil that has been spritzed with cooking spray; bring the edges of the foil up slightly around the bread to hold in place. In a bowl, beat 2 large eggs with 2 tsp. cinnamon-sugar and slowly pour the mixture over the bread cubes, soaking as much of the bread as possible. Toss on a handful of fresh raspberries and 1 fresh peach *(diced)*. Create a packet by folding the edges of the foil together, sealing the food inside. Cook over medium-high heat of a grill or on a rack over a fire for about 5 minutes; carefully unfold the foil and cook until the eggs are set. Drizzle with melted butter and maple syrup or honey.

Great for a grab-and-go breakfast when you're heading out for the day, these are super delicious and super convenient. (No need to tell anyone they're loaded with healthy stuff.)

Oats & Zucchini A.M. Cookies

2 C. white whole wheat flour

1 C. quick-cooking oats

1 tsp. cinnamon

½ tsp. baking soda

¼ tsp. salt

1 ripe banana, mashed

¼ C. butter, softened

¾ C. brown sugar

1 egg

1 tsp. vanilla

1 C. shredded zucchini

¾ C. chopped walnuts

1 C. dark chocolate chips

Before you Go

Preheat your oven to 350°.

In a bowl, mix flour, oats, cinnamon, baking soda, and salt.

In a separate bowl, beat banana, butter, brown sugar, egg, and vanilla until nice and smooth. Stir in the dry ingredients and fold in the zucchini, walnuts, and chocolate chips.

With floured hands, roll dough into balls using a generous ⅛ cup for each; arrange on parchment paper-lined baking sheets and flatten to about ½" thick. Bake for 11 to 13 minutes, until the edges begin to turn golden brown *(middle will still be slightly soft)*. Cool on the baking sheets for 10 minutes, then transfer to a wire cooling rack.

When cool, place in an airtight container for 3 or 4 days or freeze.

At Camp

Warm them up if you'd like a hot-from-the-oven cookie. Otherwise, just grab and go!

Apple Bites

Slice crisp apples into thick rounds (rounds give you more surface area for yummy toppings). Smear with marshmallow cream or nut or seed butter (PB and hazelnut are great, but try cashew or cookie butter, sunflower spread, or tahini). Add toppings like nuts, seeds, chocolate chips, dried fruit, and/or coconut and drizzle with honey or agave syrup if you'd like.

Skillet Kielbasa Hash

Olive oil

1 (14 oz.) pkg. turkey kielbasa, sliced into ¼" rounds

1 green bell pepper, diced

½ red bell pepper, diced

1 small sweet onion, diced

Salt and black pepper to taste

NEEDED AT CAMP

2 large Yukon gold potatoes

Canola oil

Salt and black pepper

Before you Go

Heat 1 tablespoon oil in a skillet; add the kielbasa and fry for 5 minutes, shaking the skillet a time or two to brown evenly. Transfer the kielbasa to a paper towel-lined plate to drain. Add the diced veggies to the skillet, season with salt and pepper, and cook until crisp-tender, stirring occasionally; transfer to the plate with the kielbasa and let everything cool.

Put the kielbasa and veggies together in a covered container and chill.

At Camp

Dice the potatoes. In a heavy skillet over a fire or on a grill, heat 2 tablespoons oil over medium-high heat. Add the potatoes and season with salt and pepper. Fry until golden brown, stirring a few times to brown evenly. Add the chilled kielbasa and veggie mixture, toss to combine, and heat through.

Bacon. It makes everybody happy and it goes with just about everything. Top these baked sweet potatoes with the crumbled salty bits and watch for smiles all around.

Maple-Bacon Sweet Potatoes

At Camp: Tightly wrap 4 medium sweet potatoes in foil and set on a rack over medium-low heat over a fire or on a grill until tender *(this could take between 45 to 70 minutes)*, turning occasionally. Meanwhile, cook and crumble 4 to 8 bacon strips; set aside. Unwrap the potatoes and cut a big "X" in the top; push together the ends and fluff the inside with a fork. Top each with butter, sour cream, maple syrup, and the crumbled bacon.

Whether you call these little gems Hen in a Nest, Spit in the Eye, Egg in a Hole, or some other clever name, this breakfast will be a winner with the kids. And the kids at heart.

Peek-a-Boo Eggs

At Camp: For each serving, butter both sides of a slice of Texas toast and cut a hole out of the center; set the cut-out portion aside. Set 2 or 3 slices of bacon side by side in a hot skillet and cook for a few minutes; position the bread slice on top so the bacon is under the hole. Carefully crack an egg into the hole, sprinkle with salt and black pepper, and cook until the bacon and egg are done to your liking. Cover the skillet with foil if you're cooking over the fire, or close the lid if you're using the grill. *(Toast the set-aside cut-out too – it might just be the kids' favorite part!)*

An interesting combination of ingredients, this summer salad is a nice change of pace from heavy mayo-based salads. Give it a try.

Mixed-Up Summer Salad

3 C. cubed seedless watermelon

1 C. diced cucumber

2 C. peeled & cubed jicama

1 T. finely chopped fresh mint

1 tsp. sea salt

½ C. full-fat coconut milk

1 T. lime zest

2 T. lime juice

1 T. real maple syrup

NEEDED AT CAMP

½ C. fresh blueberries

Before you Go

In a big bowl, combine the watermelon, cucumber, jicama, mint, and sea salt; cover and chill.

In a lidded container, combine the coconut milk, lime zest, lime juice, and syrup. Cover and shake to blend thoroughly; chill.

At Camp

Right before you're ready to eat, shake the coconut-lime mixture and add it to the watermelon mixture along with the blueberries; toss to combine.

Chill any leftovers and eat within a day or two.

This recipe is bursting with flavor and will become a much-loved favorite! Leftovers taste amazing and can be used in many different ways throughout your trip.

BBQ Pulled Pork Sandwiches

1 (3 lb.) boneless pork shoulder or pork loin

¼ C. salt-free seasoning blend

⅔ C. ketchup

⅔ C. apple cider

½ C. honey

1 T. minced garlic

⅓ C. apple cider vinegar

1 to 2 T. spicy brown mustard

2 tsp. Worcestershire sauce

½ tsp. onion powder

½ tsp. smoked paprika

¼ tsp. black pepper

2 T. brown sugar

NEEDED AT CAMP

Hamburger buns

Coleslaw, optional

Before you Go

Trim and discard excess fat from the pork and rub all sides of the meat with the seasoning blend. Set it in a slow cooker, cover, and cook on high for 4 hours or until cooked through.

When the pork is done, transfer it to a rimmed baking sheet and shred with a couple of forks and let cool. Put the cooled pork into a zippered plastic bag along with any juices that have accumulated on the baking sheet; chill.

To make the sauce, in a saucepan whisk together the ketchup, apple cider, honey, garlic, vinegar, mustard, Worcestershire sauce, onion powder, paprika, pepper, and brown sugar. Bring to a boil, then reduce heat and simmer 30 to 45 minutes until thickened, stirring occasionally. Remove from the heat, cool slightly, and pour into a jar with a tight-fitting lid; chill.

At Camp

Combine the shredded meat and the sauce and simply reheat to serve. Pile onto buns with coleslaw if you'd like.

Leftover Inspiration

Stir pulled pork into prepared macaroni & cheese; place some between bread slices with cheese and guacamole and grill to golden perfection; load onto tortilla chips with queso and jalapeños; toss with salad greens, diced tomatoes, and shredded cheese.

Crumbly graham cracker bottom, soft chocolate middle, and ooey-gooey toasted marshmallows on top... a s'mores lover's dream come true.

S'mores Jar Cakes

6 oz. bittersweet, semisweet, or milk chocolate

½ C. butter, softened, divided

1½ C. graham cracker crumbs

Salt

⅓ C. sugar

3 eggs

1 tsp. vanilla

⅓ C. flour

NEEDED AT CAMP

Marshmallows for toasting

Before you Go

Melt the chocolate and let it cool. Preheat the oven to 400° and spritz four wide-mouth pint mason jars with cooking spray.

Melt ¼ cup of the butter and mix it with the cracker crumbs and a pinch of salt. Divide the mixture among the prepped jars, packing down evenly. Cream the sugar with the remaining ¼ cup butter until light and fluffy. Add the eggs and beat well; beat in the vanilla. Stir in the flour and ¼ teaspoon salt until combined, then beat in the chocolate until just combined. Divide the batter evenly among the jars. Set a 9 x 13" rimmed baking pan in the oven and pour in 1½ cups water; set the jars in the water. Bake 25 minutes or until the top of the cakes are set but the middles are a little gooey.

Take the jars out of the oven and let them cool before tightening the lids.

At Camp

Toast marshmallows and push them into each jar. Enjoy!

The peaches in this recipe perfectly complement the pancakes which just happen to have the ideal amount of "lift." Speaking of lift, where's the coffee?

Camping Cakes & Peaches

2 C. flour

2 tsp. salt

2 T. sugar

1 tsp. baking soda

1 tsp. baking powder

2 C. plus 1 T. buttermilk

4 eggs, separated

NEEDED AT CAMP

4 ripe peaches

Vegetable oil

Toppings: butter, maple syrup, walnuts

Before you Go

In a 1-quart mason jar, combine the flour, salt, sugar, baking soda, and baking powder. In a separate jar, combine the buttermilk and egg yolks. Put the egg whites into a small mason jar. Tighten the lids; chill the jars that contain the eggs.

At Camp

Halve and pit the peaches and set the fruit aside. Heat a cast iron griddle or skillet over medium-low heat on a rack over a fire or on a grill; grease the griddle with oil.

Shake the jar containing the buttermilk and egg yolks until well blended and add to the jar with the dry ingredients; tighten the lid and shake until well mixed *(a few lumps are ok)*. Shake the egg whites vigorously until frothy; add to the batter, tighten the lid and shake to incorporate.

For each pancake, slowly pour ⅓ cup batter onto the hot griddle; cook until the tops begin to bubble and edges have set. Flip and cook the other side. In the meantime, grill the peaches until the fruit is caramelized; slice and serve with pancakes. Add toppings of choice.

Ahhh... Coffee

Need your coffee to start the day off right but don't have a coffee maker and don't like instant? Put your favorite ground coffee (enough for one cup) into a coffee filter; gather up the edges and tie tightly with unflavored dental floss or kitchen string to seal the coffee inside. Toss the filter into a cup filled with boiling water. Let it soak like a tea bag until it's as strong as you want (or need) it.

If the banana splits at your favorite ice cream shop were hot... and didn't include ice cream... they'd taste just like these. Customize anyway you'd like.

Banana Splits

For each banana split, slice a firm banana *(still in the peel)* lengthwise through the inner curve, cutting to – but not all the way through – the peeling under the banana. Pry open carefully and tuck in any combination of chopped strawberries, crushed pineapple, mini chocolate chips, mini marshmallows, and maraschino cherries. Wrap individually in foil and set in the fire or on a grill until everything is gooey and melted. Open carefully and dig in with a spoon. Got whipped cream? Go for it!

Serves 6

Mix and make the patties at home and you'll be able to hit the ground running at mealtime. Hooray!

Perfect Campin' Burgers

Before you Go: With your hands, mix 1 lb. ground beef, ½ lb. ground pork, 1 T. minced garlic, 2 T. Worcestershire sauce, 1 tsp. salt, and ½ tsp. black pepper until just combined; form into six even patties. Pack in a covered container with waxed paper between layers and chill.

At Camp: Cook patties on a rack over a low fire or plop them on a grill until done to your liking. Add a slice of cheddar or Monterey Jack cheese and let it melt over the burgers while you toast some buttered buns. Add your favorite condiments and enjoy.

Serves 3-4

Happy Times Skillet Nachos

Olive oil

1 C. diced tomatoes

Tortilla chips

1 (14 oz.) can black beans, drained & rinsed

1½ C. shredded cheddar cheese

3 sliced green onions

Salt, black pepper, and/or red pepper flakes

1 lime

Guacamole *(purchased or made with recipe on pg. 34)*

½ C. chopped fresh cilantro, optional

Your favorite toppings

At Camp

Preheat a cast iron skillet over medium-high heat over the campfire or on a grill and add a splash of oil.

Layer half the tomatoes in the hot skillet; add a layer of tortilla chips, and half the black beans, cheddar, and green onions; season to taste with salt, pepper, and/or red pepper flakes. Repeat layers. Cover the pan with foil and heat for 10 minutes or until the cheese is melted. While you wait, cut the lime into wedges.

Remove the skillet from the heat and top with guacamole and cilantro if using. Squeeze on lime juice and add your favorite toppings.

Quick, easy, and delicious. What more could you ask for?! It takes only a few flavor-charged ingredients to make these taste anything but simple.

Hawaiian Hot-Wiches

At Camp: Split 4 potato rolls. On the bottom half, stack some deli ham, a pineapple ring, and a slice of Swiss or cheddar cheese; sprinkle each with about 1 T. brown sugar and drizzle on a little Dijon mustard. Add the top half of the roll and wrap each sandwich tightly in foil; set on a rack above the fire or on the grill until nice and hot. Unwrap carefully and enjoy.

Makes 4 dozen

Are you craving something chocolate-y? Want a quick, fun, and delicious activity? Make some no-bake cookies!! They're a snap to make at the campground, and you'll have plenty to share.

Toffee No-Bake Cookies

At Camp: In a big saucepan on the grill or over a fire, combine 1 C. sugar and 1 C. light corn syrup and bring to a full boil. Remove from the heat and add 1 C. creamy peanut butter and 1 C. semisweet chocolate chips, stirring until fully melted. Stir in 3 C. quick-cooking oats, 1½ C. toffee bits, and 1 C. unsweetened flaked coconut until fully combined. Drop by rounded tablespoonful onto parchment paper or cookie sheets and let cool for 20 minutes or so. Store in an airtight container.

Dutch Oven Cornbread

½ C. flour
½ C. sugar
2 tsp. salt
½ tsp. baking soda
1½ C. yellow cornmeal

NEEDED AT CAMP
1 C. buttermilk
2 T. butter
2 eggs, beaten
1 C. milk
Toppings: butter, honey or syrup

Before you Go

In a lidded container, combine the flour, sugar, salt, baking soda, and cornmeal.

At Camp

Add the buttermilk to the flour mixture and stir to blend. Melt the butter and add to the bowl. Whisk in the eggs and milk. Pour the batter into a greased 10" Dutch oven and set it on a ring of 7 hot coals; put 15 hot coals on the lid and bake for 35 to 45 minutes, until a toothpick comes out clean, rotating the pot and lid a few times. Near the end of cooking time, move a few coals toward the center of the lid to help with browning.

Cornbread tastes great with chili (see page 36) but also makes a yummy breakfast or snack.

Extraordinary Dogs

Bow WOW
fire-roasted salsa, corn, carrot, Canadian bacon, Parmesan, and shoestring potatoes piled on a hot dog

HOT Dawg
bacon, black beans, red bell pepper, hot sauce, and mustard layered on a hot dog

Garden Pup
cucumber, radishes, green onion, and ranch dressing heaped on a hot dog

Canine Kraut
tomato, sauerkraut, avocado, and mayo smothering a hot dog